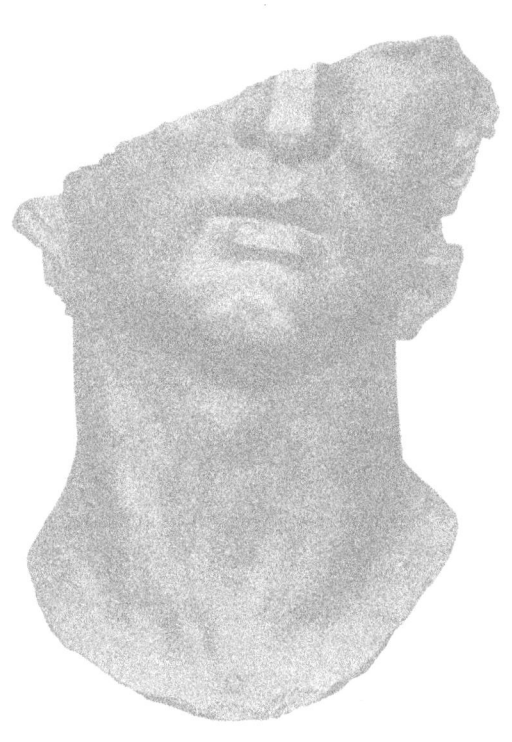

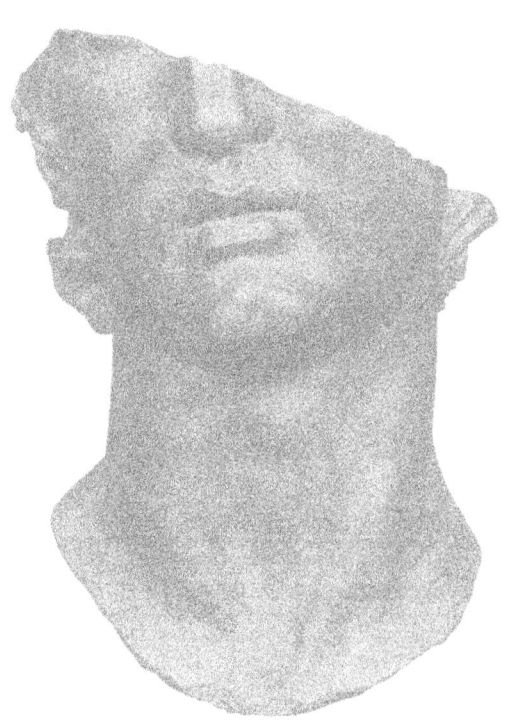

Bury Me in Cherry Blossoms

POEMS BY ERIC BRAMAN

Cirque Press

Copyright © 2024 Eric Braman

All rights reserved. No part of this publication may be reproduced, distributed or transmitted in any form or by any means, including photocopying, recording, or other electronic or mechanical methods, without the prior written permission of the publisher and author, except in the case of brief quotations embodied in critical reviews and certain other noncommercial uses permitted by copyright law.

Published by
Cirque Press

Sandra Kleven — Michael Burwell
Editors and Publishers
3157 Bettles Bay Loop
Anchorage, AK 99515

Print ISBN: 9798895466421

cirquejournal@gmail.com
www.cirquejournal.com

Cover art and design Dale Champlin
Graphic design Dale Champlin
Author photo Athena Delene

Bury Me in Cherry Blossoms

POEMS BY ERIC BRAMAN

For Kris

I love you
from Bear Mountain
to Berlin
and back again

Table of Contents

Hydrangea

I. Elm

Toothbrush	3
A Disjointed Chronicle of Coming Out	6
Learning to Drive	9
I-5 South (on Cruise Control)	12
Anxiety in Ackley, Part I	13
Anxiety in Ackley, Part II	14
Anxiety in Ackley, Part III	15
Anxiety in Ackley (and Me)	16
Squirrel in the Wall	17
Carrying Cats	19

II. Fern

Floating Over Mariana Trench	23
Grey or Blue	24
Memories of Cool Waters	25
Honey	26
Names in Sand	27
Drinking Violets	28
Pomegranate Vodka	29
Rolling Swarm	31
Sharp/Soft	32
Embers in Newberry	33
Red Roofs	34
An Inseparable Knot	35

III. Chamomile

Alaskan Lichen	42
Halfway Up Bear Mountain	43
If I Could, I Would	46
Morning Routine (A)	49
Morning Routine (B)	50
Morning Routine (C)	51
Morning Routine (D)	52
Morning Routine (E)	53
Morning Routine (F)	54
Morning Routine (G)	55

IV. Willow

BFG of Brissette Beach	59
The Scent of Sweet	61
Tap Tap Tap	63
Too Many	66
To Be Tender	67
Flavors of Sadness	68
Rug Cleaner (a YouTube Retrospect)	69
You – Limitless – You	70
Show Me Your Sadness	71
As You Have Been by Mine	72

V. Cherry

Somewhere Down	77
Yard Work in October	79
Rotting Roma in November	80
Pothos in December	82
Oxygen and Tomorrow	83
From the Poet: Hope	84
Fern Ridge (8.9.2020)	87
Bury Me in Cherry Blossoms	88

Acknowledgements	92
Appreciations	94
About the Poet	96

Hydrangea

our hydrangea grew back blue this year
and as nature always reminds us
it is never too late to change

I. Elm

*let me be an elm – growing
deep and wide / tall and proud
arms reaching for heaven
feet sturdy in the ground*

Toothbrush

we catch eyes
in my reflection
the face of
someone I don't
know
moss and allspice
peppercorn and iron
cedar and sulfur
he left
in my mouth his
taste
I brush my teeth
to get the grime
of ghosts off
my gums
each bristle
    those words
I was raised to
understand
    suck my dick
as a threat
I don't recognize
these eyes
like driving through
cattails to reach
seawalls and sandbars
filled with grains of
    faggot
    pansy
    fairy

they pile up until
waters recede
and all I'm left
with behind my lips is
plaque built-up
on yellowed teeth
cavities from chewing on
    fruitcake
and
    sod
you taste like
Miller Lite
I could never stand
your stale flavor
but I chipped my
teeth chewing the
tough leather it
takes to
    be a man
I brush with
artificial mint
trying to cover
the flavor of
fir needles and
autumn leaves
I'm not the man
my reflection
thought I would be
I brush
and brush
and brush
until I bleed

iron and rust
    man up
lava rock and gasoline
    man up
you tell me
you thought I was stronger
as I scrape the roots
expose my nerves
I brush until
I have no teeth left
I brush so hard
the words fall out
one at a time
bloodstains swirling
down the drain
and my reflection
wonders
how to
    swallow
the truth with
no teeth

A Disjointed Chronicle of Coming Out

to myself
to myself
to you
to myself

upstairs
downstairs
on the stairs
where there were no stairs

one-on-one
to a crowd
at the office
in the classroom

over a beer
under the stars
outside a bar
inside his arms

at a kitchen table
in the hall
sitting shotgun
on a swing

outside your bedroom
(in secrecy)
in the family room
(on accident)

while drunk
while high
while sober
while alone

over email
over text
in a private Facebook post
in a public Facebook post

before dinner
during dinner
after dinner
on a night no one ate dinner

before I had the words
once I had the words
after I lost the words
when the words didn't matter

in winter, while bundled
in summer, while swimming
in spring, while naked
in fall, while... getting naked

with tears in my eyes
with a smile on my face
with a knot in my stomach
with spinach in my teeth

fifteen years ago
yesterday
today
now

my god
if I could count the ways
and the places
and the people

and the times
I told myself
and then told myself
to keep quiet

my god
if I could count the times
I said, *my God*,
my god

to myself
to myself
to you
to myself

Learning to Drive

I used to mix CDs with
flavors ranging from
cayenne to vanilla.
They filled a book in
my sidekick footwell.
Sharpie-etched surfaces
read a message to readers:
"Beware s/he who listens."

I never understood how
to follow heartache
with hard rock, but with
water-filled eyes I cast
a net, pulling sonnet
and virus from the dark
web. I learned to drive
by sliding cars into ditches.

I used A/C in winter cuz
it was easier than taking
off my coat. In summer
I lost sunglasses in
glove compartments
and let gummies melt
across my dashboard. My
car collected my mistakes.

I had CDs I only played
when I drove alone. I don't
remember what songs

were in the mix, but I
recall the shame of them.
Seventeen tracks for
seventeen years I
didn't like myself,

but I pretended to.
I learned to drive by
running stop signs
and T-boning fragile
elders in larger cars,
by smashing face-first
into airbag and crying
on curbsides. I hated

myself and didn't know
how to keep my eyes
on the road while
changing channels. One
time I drank bad beer
in the basement of
someone's house I
barely knew. He played

a song on my secret CD.
I drove my car into a
traffic sign and learned
I hated myself, but should

improve my driving. I was
seventeen and I pretended
with CDs in footwells and
eyes barely on the road.

I learned to drive by
plowing through snow drifts
and hitting the brakes too
hard. I just remembered
Nora Jones was on my
secret CD. I pretended I
didn't hate myself. Over time
I got better at driving.

I-5 South (on Cruise Control)

The smoke in the sky
makes the landscape seem like
a distant memory, the details
faded (borderline greyscale),
like maybe this highway is
from a daydream, or this
hatchback is one from another
time, or maybe this journey
south is simply a step into
purgatory; no destination to
reach except the final image
of some life lived (too long or
too short / to the fullest or
overly cautious).

For once I'm running on time
and I wonder how to fit this
into the metaphor of a journey
well-traveled, or maybe a destination
can simply be reached because
I intended to get there.

No map on my dashboard nor
foot on the pedal; I'm driving with
faith in cruise control and trust
in memory—memory in
moving pictures (misted and muted).

Anxiety in Ackley, Part I

There was a sadness that hit me today and,
I think,
it also hit my dog.
The fireworks pop too loudly in
a house that feels
far too empty.
His rapid breath plays juxtaposition
to my tired eyes.
His howls between jowls shiver
in the summer heat.
I think we're both just
done with
whatever it is we're dealing with
and we don't know
how to help each other.
So, I give him a doggy downer and decide
I'll write a poem
to pass the hour when medication will kick in.

It's the Fourth of July
and neither of us are much happier
than the third.

Anxiety in Ackley, Part II

Every Fourth he gets like this:
panting, pacing, pawing,
wishing to be anywhere but here.
You're okay.
You're just fine.
I'm right here.
You're okay.
I hold him and whisper
this mantra in his ear,
but he can't hear me
over fireworks and fear.

Anxiety in Ackley, Part III

He stares at us from
just beyond the coffee table,
a small yowl
so tiny it barely travels two feet
and while I cannot hear it
I can feel it –
like his nails
(too long since last we trimmed)
scraping across the skin of my arm.
He has a way of infecting the room
with his ferment.
We check water, food, toy, but
nothing cures his ills.

Eventually the
cold and silent garage
calls him, where he lays among
Goodwill donations,
Christmas decorations,
and expired medications –
a nest to reset / relax.

His scratch to return
comes just as we press play
(every time)
like he planned this dance –

choreographed unrest.

Anxiety in Ackley (and Me)

we sigh together –
deep diaphragm pulls
under ribcaged
tensions and tethers

I run them over –
failed conversation and
missed meeting, then I
look over at his lump

eyes wide and white –
he's caught in something too
a cycle or story we don't
have language to share

we sigh together –
pulling the same air to fix
things we cannot resolve
yet find solace in knowing

we are not alone –

Squirrel in the Wall

A squirrel lives in my wall.
I hear it at midnight
scratching gently
on the sheetrock.
It's making a nest.
It's eating a grub.
I imagine its
eyes are black,
paws are clenched,
tail is flicking –
constantly flicking.

It waits
for the moment I'm
nearly asleep;
this is when
it moves.

My eyes stare hard
into the dark of
an empty ceiling.
Its trail is burned
into my brain:
forward
    (pause)
left – straight – right
    (pause)
dig – scratch – scratch
    (pause)
forward – right
    (pause)

A squirrel lives
in my wall.
You can't hear it now,
but I know
it's there.
It's watching
me.

My foot draws circles
in the sheets
wondering if when
it dies
will it rot
in the small
space between
sheetrock
and siding,
electrical wire
and support beam?

One night
I won't sleep
waiting…
waiting…
waiting…
for the scutter.

Carrying Cats

    we are
    all of us
    carrying cats
    in our crates

II. *Fern*

how our fingers u n f u r l fernlike
in   a   l o o s e n i n g   spiral
catching raindrops – drinking autumn
how they l o n g
                  l o n g to be held

Floating Over Mariana Trench
for Cullen

we made it here
one moonlit seasick night
after the other
following moon tide and tidal wave
as we ventured out into the
deep green
and here we are
35,814 feet from solid ground
and here we float
eyes pointed toward a million suns
palms placed patiently in the seafoam
ears pooling with water as we lay
weightless
imagining how much must exist
below and above
to hold us here
right here
in balance

it took courage to arrive
it will take courage to depart
the only question is
which way will we go?

Grey or Blue

a tiny house sat perched upon an isolated island
its foundation: basalt and seashells
its front porch: low tide
its address: somewhere in the great green

we set sail with intentions of
escaping / running away / watching
sunrise from the kitchen nook
sunset from the sitting room

we built a nest of knit scarves
snuggled in as the morning mist
rolled in and dreamed of growing spikes
like sea urchins securing themselves
to nearby ocean cliffs – declaring
this little land of bedsheets our
chai tea haven

we wished for forever on that island
and found it in the lines of our palms

we built seawalls to keep rising waters at bay
we distilled raindrops into the sweetest gin
we dressed ourselves in sea kelp and sea foam
we found all we needed in our tiny circle
we gave all we had to our little family

we felt happy
grey or blue
we felt happy

Memories of Cool Waters

We wash up like
dead carp on the beach,
our skin crisp in the humid heat.
We watch as our scales turn
to flakes in the summer sun.

My insides feel like gelatin
now that we're here and
I sense a seagull eying the
bloat of my belly. It's June
and I miss the cool lake water

where seaweed tickled our
tummies as we danced between
anchor and shipwreck in search
of new corners to call home.
How distant those waters feel now.

I am wafer and poison casting stench
toward sandcastle and bonfire.
You are gag reflex and warm Bud Light.
We are one *watch your step* from
being buried deep in the hot, hot sand.

It's July and I hear fireworks in the distance.
We lay stagnant, supper for sand beetles.

Honey

tannin on the tongue
it pops and snaps
as I open for a yawn
summer time lawn
so long since
last it rained
cactus mouth
dust bunny breath
saliva gone

I feel
each taste bud
canyon carved
in desert floor

parched
and wishing
for honey
on chapped lips

Names in Sand

we draw our names in the sand
knowing they will only last
as long as the wind is strong

Drinking Violets

we drink violets in fistfuls
velveteen words wrapped
in satin sentiments

finding our fill with sweets
until every petal is plucked
and we wait – wait – wait

for the next bloom

Pomegranate Vodka

for Phillip

We tasted like
pomegranate vodka
and the moonlight
on a cloudy night.
We scuffled for each other
in the shadows of a basement
with rafters covered in bedsheets.
Our bodies were stripped of façades,
hazy in our college stupor.

The vodka evaporated from
the sweat on our temples
as snow fell outside;
we warmed the room
with the friction of our fumbles.
Your freckles glowed
like lightning bugs
dancing in the forests of Kentucky.
I never told you
how much they helped me see
the pieces of myself
I hid from view
in the sobriety of daytime.

I liked the chills I got
when you stole the quilt
in the middle of the night
and mumbled curious words
from conversations in your dreams.

I guess
I loved
how
temporary
it all
was.

I can't drink
pomegranate vodka
these days;
my stomach churns at the taste,
yet my heart warms
at the scent.
I suppose some memories
soften with time,
though our stupor
never held hard edges.

Your face
looks younger each year
as you appear in my dreams
reminding me of days
I didn't know how to love someone
without vodka in my veins
and pomegranate on my breath.

Rolling Swarm

for Issa

like a rolling swarm I walked
upon your progress, one step
turned to two

Sharp/Soft

lungs filled with lavender
speak sweet sentiments
like citrus on the tongue

Embers in Newberry

we lean into one another
like logs to a fire
giving bits of ourselves
over to the heat
each touch of the other
a layer to burn
falling ashward together
we glow radiant

Red Roofs

    feathers from cardinals
    spew in the wind –
    speckles in garnet

    we follow where
    they catch

    mountain to valley
    river to seaside –
    past to present

An Inseparable Knot

I.
I think love
tastes like fifth grade
when I balanced on the edge
of my best friend's kitchen sink
sneaking sips of whiskey
from his stepdad's pantry.
We winced and grimaced,
smiled broad and weird
and said, *it's good,*
too ashamed to admit
our first taste of liquor
was anything but tasty.
Perhaps love tastes like
going back to his bedroom
to play Crash Bandicoot
with eyes a little glossier
and cheeks a little rosier.
Cheeks rosy, like
the first time I held onto his waist
when I rode behind him
on his Seadoo across
the waves of Saginaw Bay,
my stomach doing flips
before we even hit the surf,
unsure of how close to sit
or how to grasp his life jacket
without being too obvious,
wishing we could ride that Seadoo
forever
with him in front of me
and my arms around him.

II.
I think love
tastes like high school
when the only drink we could
get for the party was
cheap whiskey with no chaser.
We passed the bottle back
and forth as he said,
This is the worst shit
I've ever tasted.
I just laughed and took
another swig, gagged,
and let the heat of the
poison slide down my spine.
Maybe love tastes like
stumbling toward the campfire
with eyes crossed and
the sky above us spinning.
The world always spun
when he was near
because he looked into my eyes
when I told him stories,
and he laughed at my jokes
from a place that was deep
in his chest,
like maybe from his heart,
and I knew we'd never kiss,
but I thought of him each time
I met someone else's lips,
no matter who she was
or how long she called me
her boyfriend.

III.
I think love
tastes like college,
like Junior year when
he turned twenty-one
and I bought him a shot
of Jameson.
I didn't like whiskey, really,
but I agreed to take it with him
because he said he loved it,
because he said it was his favorite.
Our glasses clinked,
we tapped the bar,
and shot it back,
gasping for air
or at least a sip of Diet Coke.
I wonder if love
tastes like the neon lights
and rippling bass
of the dance floor,
or how I held him close
as our favorite divas sang
in fast forward and time
stretched until it nearly
stopped
because he was near
and I did not care who
saw us kiss
because he tasted like whiskey
and sex.

IV.
I think love
tastes like tonight
when he picked up the
crystal wedding decanter
and poured me a glass
of that expensive stuff,
the whiskey I got him
for Christmas.
We sat on the couch,
my hand on his knee
and head on his shoulder,
as we watched Game of Thrones
and HBO reruns.
I'm pretty sure love
tastes like right now,
with the dogs running
about the living room,
their tails wagging in the air,
and him pausing the show,
setting aside his drink,
and tossing around toys,
orchestrating a chaotic dance
of growls and yips
until they're too tired to play
and we all curl up in bed –
a shot of whiskey in our bellies
and our bodies wrapped in
an inseparable knot.

III. Chamomile

I've come to understand chamomile
the way it wafts in on a Wednesday
with the sway of a sun-kissed kitten

how it's like goldenrod in a garden
the hold of my grandmother's hand
silken and warm and soft and wise

its steam swirling in afternoon sun
silvered in slivers / cupped in palms
an autumn walk among aspen trees

how I become a grub in the ground
curled up in comfort as snow blows
beyond the blanket of fallen leaves

I've found the sips soften my edges
until I'm an ocean-tossed stone all
salt all lemon all sunset all summer

Alaskan Lichen

we woke to a fresh layer
of silver snow casting blue
light over our bedsheets

your smirk held the curve
of a black pine branch
under the weight of winter

my heart beat like a moose
calf tap-dancing down
the center of G Street

I can't recall the day, but I
know it was winter when
I decided you were a rock

and I was lichen ready
to wrap myself slowly
around each part of you

Halfway Up Bear Mountain

Halfway up Bear Mountain
I find my feet taking root into
the moss and stone, latching onto
each trailhead and viewpoint.
In Alaska it feels like we could
climb forever and never
reach the top, like the only
limit to what we could become
is our own endurance.

You're in better shape than me.

Halfway up Bear Mountain
I need to stop for a breather.
This altitude is so new to me.
I was raised in flat valleys where
water was never more than a few
meters dig beneath the feet.
I wonder aloud at the miracle
of mountains creating streams
and small falls from nowhere.

You and I know such different worlds.

Halfway up Bear Mountain
you stand perched upon a boulder,
your thumbs tucked tenderly
under the straps of your
drawstring bag, grinning
in your gray sweatshirt, unfazed,

like your heart wasn't racing,
like your head has always felt
this light in elevation.

My head is in the clouds, and yours?

Halfway up Bear Mountain
you point to a place where
lichen grows lime green against
dark purple ashen stone with
a wonder and excitement
that brightens the pink that
perches there atop your cheek
and I wonder how high I could
climb with you by my side.

I realize my whole face is fuchsia.

Halfway up Bear Mountain
I question if I ran away – all
this way – to Alaska to find you,
to reach vistas and valleys filled
with salmonberry and sweetness,
glacier water and wonderment,
if all my writing would be love
poems from now on or if you're
just a breeze passing through.

I'd stand in your wind all day.

Halfway up Bear Mountain
I kiss you on the lips. We
take a picture on my digital camera;
we don't have smart phones yet,
just Goodwill sweatshirts and
food stamp PB&Js. We walk
without questioning what
all this means as each blade
of golden grass sings in the wind.

If I Could, I Would

How do I capture these moments
of cattails and mulled wine?
How do I pause the passing clouds
so the moon stays bright in your eyes?
How do I halt the hurtling
weight of time
to remain here,
right now,
with you?

If I could, I would summon the sun
directly out of the horizon;
I'd pull it back to that
exact moment of sunset
when the fuchsia in the sky
brought out the pink in your cheeks.

If I could, I would pluck the quiet
stars from the sky and
mix them into our wine
until it sparkled
– effervescent –
bright as our eyes
the first time we kissed,
soft as our skin
secure in the sheets,
crisp as the creases
of your lips
when you laugh.

If I could, I would catch the breeze
and wrap it around us
like a wool blanket,
pulling our bodies closer and closer
until our chests are pressed
so tightly we forget what separates
our souls,
until we can't hold ourselves
from falling so deeply
into one another
that our bodies
become an afterthought.

If I could, I would imprint
every millisecond of my
life with you into a gallery
of moments,
into a display of laughter and tears,
heartache and heartbeats,
kisses and noses and fingers and hair.
I'd preserve each flash of memory
so I could never lose you,
so I could look back
and swim through a sea
of every moment that showed me
why the sun rises
each day
and why
mountains reach
for the sky.

If I could, I would rub the ink
of this poem into my skin
until it sinks into my bloodstream,
pumps through my being,
and merges with my DNA
so I always remember
how to love,
how to stay still,
how to look into the horizon
and dream of stardust and spaceships.

If I could, I would.
I would save you.
Every moment of you.
Every moment of this world with you,
I would.

In the meantime,
I'll do my best
to absorb you like a sponge
and hold you in my pores,
to never let this feeling
of saturation
evaporate.

Morning Routine (A)

on sunday
we wake up
    (when we want to)
with your arms
around my waist

we lay there
    (breathing)
until the dogs scratch the door
enough to make us
    get up
    stretch the rubber bands
    in our backs
and make coffee

I like sundays

Morning Routine (B)

on monday
>I wake to the sound
>of my fourth alarm
>and the door closing
>behind you
>leaving for work

the dogs snore
as I waste time
reading click bait
>(in my underwear)

until there's only
ten minutes left
to brush my teeth
>(and maybe shower)

Morning Routine (C)

on tuesday
the sky is grey
but the bed is warm

(you don't work until ten)
so I roll over
and wrap my arms
around your waist
    we lay
        like two tangled noodles
        floating in a pot
until I need to shower
or you crave your coffee fix

Morning Routine (D)

    on wednesday
           neither of us want
           to get up
    so we play tag
    seeing who can
    press snooze the longest
        (I win)

    the only thing
    that lifts me out of bed
    is the smell of coffee
        (you brewed)
    and the dogs
        needing to pee
        needing to pee
        needing to pee

Morning Routine (E)

on thursday
we both have
early meetings

you beat me to the shower

the dogs and I
exchange tired looks
      as I
      (half asleep)
      watch minutes
      slowly pass

you step into the room
      (steamy and naked)
and for a moment
I wish we could call in sick
to tussle our fresh skin
in these wrinkled sheets

I walk past
grazing one finger
against your hip
two quiet trains passing
in the twilight of morning

Morning Routine (F)

on friday
we press snooze
at the same time
our sheets smell
of wine-stale drool
      (syrah from last night)

the bags under our eyes
tell the tale of
thirty-somethings
learning their
bodies
have
changed

we go back to sleep
knowing in ten minutes
we'll share the ritual
      (again)

Morning Routine (G)

on saturday
we don't set alarms
we let ourselves rise
to the scutter of
clawed feet
across hardwood floors
and dog tags jingling
like christmas bells

you wake before me
    (I notice)
but you don't disturb me
    until
        you're hungry
        for pancakes

I don't want to get up
but I do for you
    and
    because
    (I also want pancakes)

IV. *Willow*

*we wept with the willow –
in the heat of a too-long summer*

*our tears like autumn leaves
fell into the bay / her waves
reaching seawalls she once
loved with hands too heavy*

*summer used to be cooler
– when the willow wept with us*

BFG of Brissette Beach

it was a willow tree that defined the
skyline of my childhood – its silken
branches danced with the breeze
and whipped with the offshore winds

water once sat at the roots with an
accumulation of seaweed and the
rib bones of rotten carp – we used
to swing into such putrid sludge

it stood upon white stones, boulder,
and soft sand – yet somehow it held
on, even as a tornado jumped from
cattail-filled marsh to blustering bay

once, a crowbar fell from its branches
onto my brother's head – the mistake
of an absent-minded teenager trying
to construct a mini mansion in the sky

I tried to complete the task once I was
old enough to climb its trunk – instead
I ate Swiss Cake Rolls and drank Sprite
in the skeleton of a half-built tree home

this Big Friendly Giant was cut down
yesterday – and I just don't know how
we'll navigate boats back to shore
without this bayside beacon to follow

my mother will plant a new tree, she'll
water it with the tears of saying goodbye
to a dearly departed arbor – I know we
won't live to see the day it fills the sky

yet I see it now: a giggling child
swinging from willow whip to seaweed
slime – there on the same real estate,
but from the branches of another giant

The Scent of Sweet

our bathroom counter is a sugar ant highway
little legs traverse false marble
in search of something sweet
t h e y   w a n d e r
drawn by the false promises
of hand soaps and toothpaste
a pale peach olfactory mirage
where dust and scum texture
the path beneath their feet
but somewhere something sweet
                         pulls them forward

a layer of skin from my dry hand
swirls in the basin
as I lose track of my washing
trying to place wherever it is they
are coming from
nowhere, really, it seems
they are wanderers
s e e k e r s
lost in the flow of following what feels right
in a place that I'm certain
                         is wrong

one crawls into the bowl of the sink
and without thought I turn my hand
into a waterslide
creating a river to wash the little speck
                         down the drain

a twinge of sadness creeps in
from the corners and cracks of the room
l i t t l e   s o l d i e r s
in search of
something lost

                                          someone lost

traveling what must be
s o   f a r
for things
s o   s m a l l
and I wonder
will they get distracted
by something sweet

                                    or travel
                                    down
                                    the drain
                                    seeking
                                    the source
                                    of sewer-bound
                                    cries

I re-lather my hands
to rid the smell of
crushed ant

                                    and lost thought

may this lavender
cleanse me of
m y   s i n s

Tap Tap Tap

I fell out of myself
landed on the ceiling
stared down at a place
I once called home

find my spine feel it
crawl up my back
where does my breath
live where are my lungs

tap tap tap the pieces
of me I can still reach
skin skin skin on my arms
my legs my hands my face

I remember flying from
dorm beds to bathrooms
landing in showers and
forgetting what room was mine

he always tasted like beer
or Burnettes – sometimes pot
or stale cigarettes ashtray
on the tongue I never enjoyed

his taste still in my mouth
when I woke unsure of hour
or final hours of my time with
him him him me me me

tap tap tap the pieces of me
I can still reach anything that
reminds me I am still here
still seated or standing or something

that reminds me I have a body
to call home / home to call
like my body that I live in
it's Tuesday – it's Tuesday

tap tap tap touch touch touch
the pieces of me I can reach
the parts I can forgive the pieces
I can look in the face face face

tap tap tap into the moments
I fear most the facts facts facts
I pushed aside for all these years
you you you who I hurt who hurt

me me me it was me me me
who was so silent for so long
tap tap tap touch touch touch
be be be here here here

return to the body the one
I call home return to now now now
to today to Tuesday to this couch
to these lungs to this spine

tap tap tap
touch touch touch
heal heal heal
return – forgive

Too Many

the number of poems
I've started with I

if I could only remove
myself from these feelings

breathe between each word
fill lung with metaphor

and exhale stanzas
that place the world

in couplets
myself within it

but not so in it
that I can't escape it

To Be Tender

1. mix one-part baking soda with one-part self

2. take hammer to raw meat and flatten the muscle until it resembles cardstock and felt

3. use hand and nail to massage each fiber until it softens or each finger is coated in the feeling that maybe this breast looked better before beating it down

4. regret something and hesitate to wash away its residue

5. lose ability to season or turn oven knob without spreading the slime

6. wish to go back – to return to a time when breast was firm and lemon pepper kissed the nostrils, tempting one to never touch the muscle in the first place

7. act and regret

8. to be tender, one must

9. regret

Flavors of Sadness

lavender, cold coffee,
tuesday afternoon,
mealy tomato, sage,
candle wax, chlorine,
frayed canvas thread,
gas station hot dog,
dark chocolate, dust,
vodka soda, aspirin,
ocean mist, rainfall,
morning breath, rust
birthday cake, cattail,
cerulean blue, pine,
swing set, Reese's,
musty hymnal, you,
and me

Rug Cleaner (a YouTube Retrospect)

I get lost in another video
of a soiled rug, long forgotten
in a garden, being washed.

There is something soothing
in the grey-brown foam washing
away to reveal cerulean below.

Just a scrub, just a watering can
of sanitizer, just some bristles
to make it look good as new.

Like Thursday showers trying to
scrub bags from under my eyes;
hot water to scald and scour.

Or Sunday baths with wine in
hand – I just need to soak a bit,
let loose the soil and give up

the toxic bits I've locked in
my stitch. Don't scrub too hard.
I fear I'll unwind or tangle myself

into the rotary trying its best to
make me clean again. Perhaps
all I need is a sound night's sleep.

I turn on YouTube, binge on videos
that scratch the surface of all
the cleaning that needs to be done.

You – Limitless – You

Car sitting, consuming what news
is served by NPR, when suddenly
I hear the pronoun *they* used to
describe a singular person. My
sibling, seen fully in their never-
binaried wonder. I feel the cool
embrace of every Queer person
on this planet wrap around my skin
as the hairs raise on my arms
knowing that this reporter asked,
And what pronouns did they use?
Dignity in death, honored in national
headlines. You were one of us – a
cumulonimbus cloud filling vacant
sky, a particle of dust catching light
making mudroom sparkle, bubbles
in a bath holding lavender oil on
your surface.

How strange to feel seen in this
moment of tragedy. How terrible
for death to be an affirmation. How
awful to know I'll never know you.

you – limitless – you

Show Me Your Sadness

Throw it like marinara at the wall,
handfuls at a time – let it splash
until every inch of this room is
covered in red.

Dump it like dead houseplants from
chipped pottery – let the soil fall
like last night's tears onto the rug in
piles and piles.

Spatter it like toothpaste foam on
the bathroom mirror – no regard for
the reflection staring back at your
brilliant mess.

Reveal every inch of you wishing
to burst – tell me where your skin
burns and your heart hurts so I can
layer with lavender.

And here is mine, tiny cactus spines
on fresh fingertips – I know these parts prefer
to blossom at night, so let's not be alone
as the petals appear.

As You Have Been by Mine

for the Vances

When the clouds hang low covering the treetops
and mountain peaks let me be your clear skies
shining sun upon your face. Let me burn through
the morning mist and greet you with a soft
embrace. Let me warm your skin
until your bones no longer shiver,
until you're pink in the face,
until the bees leave their nest.

If you need courage, friend, let me collect
the most resilient ferns in the forest
bursting through the charred ground reminding
blackened tree trunks that after every fire
comes life. Let me sew these ferns into a castle,
for you to sit at the throne breathing their spores
until your DNA unfurls,
until your spine grows straight,
until your kingdom come.

If you need strength let me pull at the fibers
of my muscle like loose strings unraveling
the pieces of myself onto a spool to be weaved
into blankets or armor, to warm and protect you,
to comfort and encourage you. Wrap yourself
in all that is given so it may hold you up when
it feels the wind is too strong or the demons
creep in the shadows. Use this shield
to stand firm,
to find your footing,
to move forward.

If you need love I will collect the hearts
of every mouse in the field,
of every sparrow in the sky,
of every salmon in the sea.
I'll loop them on a chain to be worn around
your neck, to rest on your chest, to soak
into your skin, to embellish you, my friend,
because you are loved beyond the capacity
of every heart I could collect,
of every poem I could write,
of every metaphor I could compile.

If you need me just say the word, just raise
your hand, because I know the road is rough,
I know the night is dark and I never want
you to think you must journey on your own.

I'm here by your side as you have been by mine.
You're here by my side as I have been by yours.
I'm here by your side as you have been by mine.

V. Cherry

seasons change
fresh fruit / orange leaf / bare branch
yet still
we remember the blossom

Somewhere Down

somewhere down
this hill I hear
gunshots

practice for
hunts or battles or war or
blasts at the hands of souls
too young to comprehend
the power in their palms

the whitetail deer in my stomach
leaps the ledge of this cliff as she
prays for a
soft landing or protection below
not knowing or understanding
how far she will fall

the jackrabbit in my heart
seeks the nearest bush
overcome with
shakes and shivers
his eyes growing wide as harvest moons

the man in the back of my mind
wonders where
(he went wrong)
to respond to the sound of
survival
with such distaste

the woman in my ribcage
wonders how
(she became so trapped)
in this toxic cycle
coursing
through my veins

I stand trapped in a trance
(conflicted)
by all the parts of me
in disagreement
on who I am meant to be

gunshots
this hill I hear
somewhere down

Yard Work in October

lace made of spider webs
strong enough to
withstand wasps
delicate enough to
break in the breeze

what I would give
to bury myself in
the fallen leaves
and hibernate through winter

Rotting Roma in November

The tomatoes were beginning
to rot, barely hanging on to
the vine after our first frost.
I tried to handle them with
care, but they burst like water
balloons in the palm of my
hand causing their sour juices
to soak into the leather gloves
and cold earth. I scooped their
skins with clumsy fingers,
holding my breath as I cleansed
the bed of debris. I remember
how fruitful this all once
was, when we were younger
and the summer sun and
hose water gave more fruit
than we could harvest. I've
had heartburn for two months
trying to eat the tomatoes and
sauces and soups of summer.
I can't say I mourn the end of
this season. Perhaps I should
have pulled them sooner, saved
the mess, but what is autumn
without a few fallen seeds?

We'll tend to the sprouts
next spring. We'll take Tums.
We'll add cream to our sauces.

We'll eat stews and salads
and feel far from the smell
of rotting Roma in November.

Pothos in December

pothos with a backdrop of snow /
one window / between warm and
cold / I consider this long vine so
foreign to the sight of sleet / did
it ever question its / place in the
kitchen / or maybe it trusts that
it is right where it is meant / to be
between fern and succulent / on
a countertop in Oregon / just all
in / and out of place at once and
maybe that is / okay.

Oxygen and Tomorrow

I'd like to exhale this past year
like I'm watching my breath
turn to steam on a cold winter day
little particles left of what fed me
and each bit of toxin I no longer need
dissipating in a cloud until
all that's left is empty lungs
ready for filling with fresh air

I'd like to enter this new year
gulping down a deep, glorious inhale
like the kind you take after
holding your breath under water
in a contest of endurance
one where I don't fear what
fleck may catch in my throat
just faith I'll pull what I need

a collective sigh at 11:59
a deep breath at midnight
a cheers to oxygen and tomorrow

From the Poet: Hope

for Mia, and now you

It's there
this... thing
this... push
to look deep
into the dark,
to find color
without light.

It's... blue
(I think)
like the
midnight sky
in July
when the moon
casts crescents
in the irises of
passersby.

It's... violet
(that's it)
like lilac in
late spring,
a sprig of
periwinkle wonder
placed gently
in the palm.

It's... green
(it must be)
like old oak
coated in moss,
filled with
story and lore
in each burst
of bright lichen.

It's... white
(ah, yes)
almost blinding
when you see it.

It's... yellow
and orange
and red
(I know)
it burns until we
believe it will
never leave.

It's... here
(always here)
and it's whatever
color we need
it to be.
It won't leave
until we ask it to,

so sit and
take in its
splendor;
let it settle
in your bones.
Let it hold you up
to Tuesday,
through Thursday,
and place you
gently in today
pointed purposefully
toward tomorrow.

It's... you
here, right now,
looking faithfully
for your future;
the rose of
your cheek and
gold of your heart
is the color –
is the color
of hope.

Fern Ridge (8.9.2020)

I can see
to the reservoir
from this height

promises we
will never run
dry, no matter

the season, but
this August the
waters look low

yet the land looks
green – evergreen
sharp to the sight

like sweet citrus
on the lips, a cool
key lime pie

on hot summer
days we dream of
autumn but this

year our dreams
are spring-ward
after the snowpack

has passed and
our reservoir is
full – full – full

Bury Me in Cherry Blossoms

when I die
bury me in cherry blossoms
preserve me in petunias
place irises upon my eyes
and crown me in carnations
let this harsh exterior
give way to
milkweed and magnolia
I could never carry the
kindness of camas
kissing the river's edge
I never found the freedom
to sprout full bloom
like fuchsia or geranium
so let my burial be a rainbow
of red roses and blue violets
yellow yarrow and white wisteria
let vines of morning glory
wrap me
cocoon me
and compost me
until I'm soil and clay
let these atoms I hold
transform and add texture
to every wildflower in this field
until my full spectrum is revealed
embedded in the faces of old friends
trillium and tiger lily
larkspur and lavender
blackberry and begonia

every petal of the alphabet
beauty and bounty
wild and wonder
full and free

bury me in cherry blossoms
remember me as
colorful as spring

Acknowledgments

"Toothbrush" was first published in Moon Tide Press's *Sh!t Men Say to Me*, released in 2021.

"Learning to Drive" was first published in High Shelf Press's *High Shelf XXXVIII*, released in January 2022.

"Floating Over Mariana Trench" was first published by Enfleshed in their digital collection, *Additional Blessings from the Deep* in 2022.

Versions of "If I Could, I Would" and "As You Have Been by Mine" were both first heard on the album *By Your Side*, a project done in collaboration with musician Cullen Vance.

"The Scent of Sweet" was first published in Cirque Press's *CIRQUE #27 Volume 14, No. 1*, released in May 2024.

"Somewhere Down" first appeared in the art installation *My Own Flag to Raise* in 2022 coordinated by Jessica Rehfield at the Focus Gallery in Salem, Oregon. It also appeared in the zine *Queer Mis-Representation* created by the Queer Zine Collective.

"From the Poet: Hope" was inspired by the poem "Hope" written by Mia Vance in her premier collection *Instead of Butterflies*. This poem was also a gift as she completed her studies at the University of Oregon.

"Fern Ridge (8.9.2020)" was first published by the Cottage Grove Harpies, appearing in *Passages*, their 2022 literary anthology.

Appreciations

Thank you, Kris, for your endless support, love, encouragement, and good looks. You somehow find ways to make me feel I'm simultaneously floating and grounded.

Thank you, Mom and Dad, for always believing in me throughout my life and ensuring my creative spark turned into a steady flame.

Thank you, Grandma, for egg sandwiches and your endless words of encouragement.

Thank you, Mia, for your advice, support, edits, friendship, and for reminding me I'm a "big fucking artist."

Thank you, Mike, Sandy, Dale and the whole Cirque Press Team, for seeing promise in this collection and supporting with valuable edits to get me over the finish line.

Additional thanks to Issa, Jaime, Michelle, Allison, Shannon, Nancy, Cullen, Melissa, Gypsy, Tara, Inga, Erica, Chelsey, Rachael, Ben, Aimee, Jorah, Theresa, Stacey, Abigail, Ritu and Kerry and the many other individuals who have encouraged and supported me through the years. I'm deeply blessed to be surrounded by such brilliance.

About the Poet

Eric Braman (they/them) is a poet, playwright, storyteller, and visual artist performing and showcasing work in the Pacific Northwest. *Bury Me in Cherry Blossoms* is Eric's premier poetry collection. Their work has appeared in publications by High Shelf Press, Moon Tide Press, Cirque Press, *Qu Literary Magazine*, *The Coachella Review*, and more. Eric was an honorarium recipient for the 2022 Oregon Fringe Festival where they premiered their original autobiographical show *To You / To Myself*. They have been seen performing on stages and their plays have been produced by theaters across the United States. Born and raised in Kawkawlin, Michigan, they currently live in Springfield, Oregon where they regularly escape into the woods to hike and write.

www.ericbraman.com

About Cirque Press

Cirque Press grew out of *Cirque*, a literary journal that publishes the works of writers and artists from the North Pacific Rim, a region that reaches north from Oregon to the Yukon Territory, south through Alaska to Hawaii, and west to the Russian Far East.

Cirque Press is a partnership of Sandra Kleven, publisher, and Michael Burwell, editor. Ten years ago, we recognized that works of talented writers in the region were going unpublished, and the Press was launched to bring those works to fruition. We publish fiction, nonfiction, and poetry, and we seek to produce art that provides a deeper understanding about the region and its cultures. The writing of our authors is significant, personal, and strong.

Sandra Kleven – Michael Burwell, publishers and editors

www.cirquejournal.com

Books From Cirque Press

Apportioning the Light by Karen Tschannen (2018)

The Lure of Impermanence by Carey Taylor (2018)

Echolocation by Kristin Berger (2018)

Like Painted Kites & Collected Works by Clifton Bates (2019)

Athabaskan Fractal: Poems of the Far North by Karla Linn Merrifield (2019)

Holy Ghost Town by Tim Sherry (2019)

Drunk on Love: Twelve Stories to Savor Responsibly by Kerry Dean Feldman (2019)

Wide Open Eyes: Surfacing from Vietnam by Paul Kirk Haeder (2020)

Silty Water People by Vivian Faith Prescott (2020)

Life Revised by Leah Stenson (2020)

Oasis Earth: Planet in Peril by Rick Steiner (2020)

The Way to Gaamaak Cove by Doug Pope (2020)

Loggers Don't Make Love by Dave Rowan (2020)

The Dream That Is Childhood by Sandra Wassilie (2020)

Seward Soundboard by Sean Ulman (2020)

The Fox Boy by Gretchen Brinck (2021)

Lily Is Leaving: Poems by Leslie Ann Fried (2021)

One Headlight by Matt Caprioli (2021)

November Reconsidered by Marc Janssen (2021)

Callie Comes of Age by Dale Champlin (2021)

Someday I'll Miss This Place Too by Dan Branch (2021)

Out There In The Out There by Jerry McDonnell (2021)

Fish the Dead Water Hard by Eric Heyne (2021)

Salt & Roses by Buffy McKay (2022)

Growing Older In This Place: A Life in Alaska's Rainforest by Margo Wasserman Waring (2022)

Kettle Dance: A Big Sky Murder by Kerry Dean Feldman (2022)

Nothing Got Broke by Larry F. Slonaker (2022)

On the Beach: Poems 2016-2021 by Alan Weltzien (2022)

Sky Changes on the Kuskokwim by Clifton Bates (2022)

Transplanted by Birgit Lennertz Sarrimanolis (2022)

Between Promise and Sadness by Joanne Townsend (2022)

Yosemite Dawning by Shauna Potocky (2022)

In the Winter of the Orange Snow by Diane S. Carpenter (2023)

The Woman Within by Tami Phelps and Kerry Dean Feldman (2023)

All in Due Time by Kate Troll (2023)

Mail Order Nurse by Sue Lium (2023)

Getting Home from Here by Anne Ward-Masterson (2023)

Crossing the Burnside Bridge & Other Poems by Janice D. Rubin (2023)

Infinite Meditations For Inspiration and Daily Practice by Scott Hanson (2023)

A Variable Sense of Things by Ron McFarland (2023)

Tiny's Stories: An Athabascan Family on the Yukon River by Theresa "Tiny" Demientieff Devlin with Sam Demientieff (2024)

If Singing Went On by Gerald Cable (2024)

May the Owl Call Again: A Return to Poet John Meade Haines, 1924-2011 by Rachel Epstein (2024)

Out of the Dark: A Memoir by Marian Elliott (2024)

Kissing Kevin: An American Nurse in the Vietnam War by Sara Berg (2024)

Boardwalk Footsteps: Memoir of an Artist at a Remote Alaskan Cannery by Dot Bardarson (2024)

A Wonderful-Terrible God by Judith Lethin (2024)

Bury Me in Cherry Blossoms by Eric Braman (2024)

Taking Time: Sailing Away with My Family in Southeast Alaska by Larri Irene Spengler (2024)

Last Call of the Dark by Mary Eliza Crane (2024)

Dancing Away by Robert M. Fagen (2024)

Lost Last Poems by Shannon Gramse (2024)

Seasmoke, Spindrift and Other Spells by Shauna Potocky (2024)

The North Face of Summer by Russell Tabbert (2024)

CIRCLES

Illustrated books from Cirque Press

Baby Abe: A Lullaby for Lincoln by Ann Chandonnet (2021)

Miss Tami, Is Today Tomorrow? by Tami Phelps (2021)

Miss Bebe Goes to America by Lynda Humphrey (2022)

More Praise for
Bury Me in Cherry Blossoms

Like the outstretched hand of a close friend, Eric's poetry unfurls and invites you to join the journey. Filled with flavorful moments and decorated with the palpable inspiration of nature, this collection will nestle easily into both your heart and your bookshelf to be enjoyed again and again.

—Melissa Rose, author of *Baggage*

Bury Me in Cherry Blossoms, like a case of fine wine, releases a bouquet of stories distilled from passion, wonder and big-hearted generosity. Eric Braman's unique voice is powered by a fierce tenderness that finds elegance in the everyday, joy in self-discovery, and resilience in heartache. These poems are grounded in a luscious sense of place, juicy and filled with the embodied joy of living and loving on earth. Eric's sensuous effervescent life-force carves out a space for the reader, begging each of us to give voice to the whirling dervish of change that is who we are. This collection is a heart-opening experience!

—Theresa May, author of *Becoming Blue Corn* and *Salmon Is Everything*

Like breathing in a bounty of blossoms, inhaling this book gifts the senses and the soul. Visceral and ethereal, Eric's writing reads itself to our ears. A clear microphone for the heart, from a poet who blends the arts of stage and page.

> —Jorah LaFleur, author of *Words for Gratitude* and *Covidian Times*

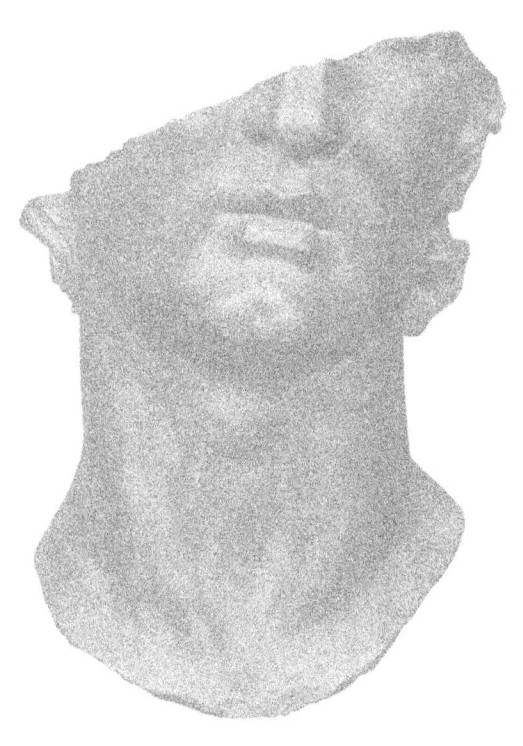

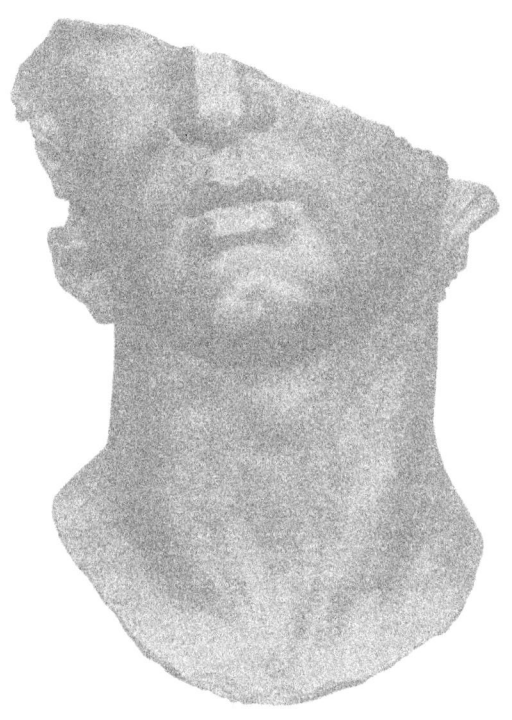

www.ingramcontent.com/pod-product-compliance
Lightning Source LLC
LaVergne TN
LVHW061618070526
838199LV00078B/7333